Classification
of Living and Nonliving Things

Elizabeth Rose

The Rosen Publishing Group's
PowerKids Press™
New York

For Flannery Emma and Emma Bean

Published in 2006 by The Rosen Publishing Group, Inc.
29 East 21st Street, New York, NY 10010

First Edition

Editor: Rachel O'Connor
Book Design: Albert B. Hanner

Photo Credits: Cover and p. 1 © Corbis; p. 5 (top) © Image Bank/Getty Images, (bottom) © Jacob Halaska/Index Stock Imagery; p. 7 (top) © Eric and David Hoskings/Corbis, (bottom) © Phil Schermeister/Corbis; p. 9 (top) © Sanford/Agliolo/Corbis, (bottom) © Frank W. Lane; Frank Lane Picture Agency/Corbis; p. 11 (top left) © Craig Tuttle/Corbis, (top right) © Ron Watts/Corbis, (bottom) © Royaltyfree/Corbis; p. 12 Joel Sartore/National Geographic Image Collection; pp. 13 (top), 15 (bottom) © Richard TT. Norwitz/Corbis; p. 13 (bottom) © Efital Photography/Animals Animals/Earth Scenes/All Rights Reserved; p. 15 (top) © John Conrad/Corbis; p. 17 © Alan Schein Photography/Corbis; p. 18 © Lester V. Bergman/Corbis; p. 19 (top) © Frank Young; Papilio/Corbis, (bottom) © Charles Philip/Corbis; pp. 21, 22 Photodisc/Getty Images.

Library of Congress Cataloging-in-Publication Data

Rose, Elizabeth, 1970–
Classification of living and nonliving things / Elizabeth Rose.
    p. cm. — (The Life science library)
Includes bibliographical references (p.   ).
Contents: Classification — Living and nonliving — Plants and animals — Sorting by parts — Sorting by homes — Sorting by diet — Nonliving parts — Scientific sorting — Sorting the five kingdoms — Sorting yourself.
ISBN 1-4042-2818-7 (lib. bdg.)
1. Biology—Classification—Juvenile literature. [1. Biology—Classification.] I. Title. II. Series.

QH83.R657 2005
570'.1'2—dc22

                                        2003023708

Manufactured in the United States of America

Contents

Classification

There are believed to be at least 10 million kinds of living things in this world. How can anyone keep track of them all? One way is through a system called classification. This is a way to keep track of things by sorting them into groups. You might have used this system to sort your CDs or your books. When you separate your books about science and your books about sports, you are sorting, or classifying, your books. Classifying the things of the world allows scientists to keep track of and study both living and nonliving things. In this book we are going to look at some ways to classify the living and nonliving things on Earth.

Here a young girl sorts jelly beans by color. She has sorted them into three colors. They are dark green, pink, and light green. You can sort any number of things in any number of ways. You may decide to sort your books, for example. You can sort them by subject, by size, by color, or by any other way that you think would be a fun way of sorting them.

Scientists study things to find out about them. Scientists sort things into groups based on the properties they share with one another.

5

Living and Nonliving

Scientists use scientific classification to sort the world, but there are many other ways of sorting. One way we can sort things is by classifying them as living or nonliving. Living things use energy. They move or change shape. They take in food and get rid of waste, and they have babies, or **reproduce**. Humans, insects, trees, and grass are living things.

Nonliving things do not move by themselves, grow, or reproduce. They exist in nature or are made by living things. There are three groups of nonliving things. They are solids, liquids, and gases. Water is an example of a liquid. A rock is a solid. **Oxygen** is an example of a gas. Cars, pencils, and air are examples of nonliving things.

Living things have babies, or reproduce. Here a golden oriole feeds its nesting young. Orioles build cup-shaped nests in which to lay their eggs. Both sexes incubate the eggs, or keep them warm.

Pictured here are rocks found by Lake Albert in Oregon. Rocks are a good example of nonliving things.

Plants and Animals

   Now let's sort the members of the group of living things into smaller groups. One way to sort living things is to separate them into plants and animals. A plant grows in a fixed place. It also has no eyes, ears, or nose, and it makes its own food. There are more than 300,000 types of plants on our planet.

   The other major group of living things in the world is the animal group. This group has about two million **species**. Animals get their food by eating living things. Most animals move around to get their food. Most animals also use their noses, eyes, and ears to sense the world around them.

Plants and trees use the energy they get from sunlight to make food in their leaves. This is a system called photosynthesis. Here we can see the sunlight shine down on a pine forest in Honshu, Japan.

Gerbils are members of the animal kingdom. They have large eyes and powerful back legs that help them spring forward. Gerbils are 3 to 5 inches (8–13 cm) long, not including their long tail. Their diet consists of nuts, roots, and grains. In recent years gerbils have become popular as house pets. They are easy to raise and are usually gentle.

Sorting by Parts

One way to classify living things is to sort them by parts. Animals can be sorted by whether they have a backbone, or spine. **Vertebrates** is the term scientists use for animals with backbones. Humans, birds, fish, and reptiles are all vertebrates. Animals without backbones are called **invertebrates**. Worms, spiders, and grasshoppers are invertebrates. Animals can also be sorted by other features. For example, a peacock and a sparrow both have feathers and breathe air. They are birds. They belong to a group called **mammals**. Plants can also be sorted by their parts. Plants with leaves go in one group. Plants with needles, such as pine trees, go in another group.

Some plants grow flowers, such as the sunflower shown here. Other plants, like the pine tree, have cones. These differences allow plants to be further sorted into groups.

The human backbone consists of 24 movable vertebrae. Vertebrae are the bony pieces that make up the spine. There are 7 cervical vertebrae found in the neck region, 12 thoracic in the midback area, and 5 lumbar vertebrae in the lower-back region.

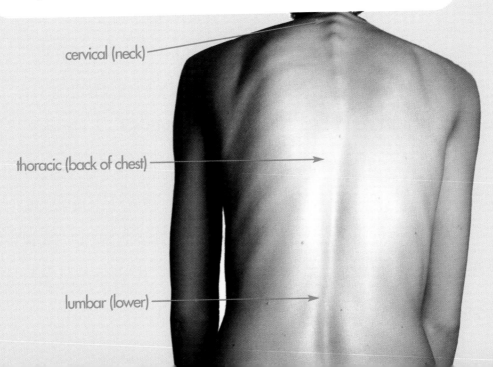

cervical (neck)

thoracic (back of chest)

lumbar (lower)

Sorting by Homes

Animals and plants can be sorted by where they live, or their **habitat**. Some animals, such as moles and earthworms, live underground. Swamp deer, alligators, and herons all live in swamps. Swamp deer have flat, wide feet. These keep the deer from sinking in the soft ground around swamps. Herons have long toes for the same reason. Animals with fins, such as dolphins and sharks, always live in water. Do you know where an animal with little or no fur and large ears might live? If you guessed a desert habitat, you are right. Large ears help an animal lose body heat and stay cool in hot weather.

Plants can be sorted by habitat. For example, a plant with a thick, waxy covering and thorns instead of leaves lives in a desert habitat. Plants lose water through their leaves. Cacti and other desert plants often have thorns instead of leaves so they do not lose as much water. This thorny cactus's waxy skin helps it save water. The cactus also loses very little water through its thorns.

Desert areas make up about one-quarter of Earth's land. The desert is home to the fennec fox. This fennec fox's giant ears do not just help it hear its prey. Its ears also help the fox lose body heat, which helps the animal stay cool in hot weather.

13

Sorting by Food

Scientists often sort animals by what they eat. **Herbivores**, for example, eat only plants. Cows and deer are examples of herbivores. **Carnivores** eat mostly meat. They usually have sharp claws and sharp pointed teeth for catching **prey** and tearing meat. Cats, dogs, and weasels are examples of carnivores. **Omnivores** eat everything. People are omnivores. So are bears, raccoons, and many birds. **Insectivores** are animals that eat insects. Hedgehogs, moles, and anteaters are types of insectivores. There is another way to sort animals by diet. Some animals eat during the day, such as horses and dogs. Others, such as bats and owls, eat at night.

Omnivores have both flat teeth for chewing plants and sharp front teeth for tearing meat. This bear will use his sharp teeth to eat the salmon he has just caught.

Herbivores have flat teeth for chewing grass and other plants. A cow has four stomachs to help it break down its meals. Pictured here is a cow eating a meal of green grass.

Nonliving Things

Sometimes it is helpful to classify nonliving things. Sorting books, clothes, or CDs will help you when you want to find something later. You can begin sorting nonliving things by deciding whether a nonliving thing is humanmade or natural. Natural things are found in nature. Humanmade things have been changed by people. A chair and a table are humanmade things.

Once you have decided whether the thing is natural or humanmade, you can sort it by its makeup. People sort nonliving things every time they sort their recycling. Things made of plastic go in one **container**. Metal goes in another. Paper goes in another, and glass goes in yet another.

Recycling helps to save natural resources, or things that occur in nature. Natural resources are necessary for life on Earth.

Scientists sort rocks into groups based on the minerals, or natural elements, that formed them. Quartz, gypsum, and azurite are examples of different types of minerals that form rocks.

Azurite   Gypsum   Quartz

Scientific Sorting

The bacterium shown here is a moneran. Like the protists, monerans are usually just one cell, but they are smaller and simpler than protists. It can be hard for scientists to decide where living things belong. They might move a living thing from one kingdom to another as they discover more about that living thing.

Scientists separate all living things in the world into five main groups, called kingdoms, in order to study them. Two of these kingdoms are the plant and animal kingdoms. Scientists also sort some living things into a kingdom called **fungi**. Fungi seem like plants because they grow in a fixed place. However, they cannot make their own food. Mushrooms are an example of fungi. Another kingdom is the protist kingdom. Protists are tiny organisms, or creatures, that are usually made of just one **cell**. The final kingdom is the moneran kingdom. Monerans are **microscopic** organisms, such as bacteria.

This orange peel fungus is a member of the fungi kingdom. It takes its name from its color and shape, which are like the peels of an orange.

Pictured here is a bullfrog covered in algae in an algae pond. Algae are plantlike living things without roots or stems that live in water. Scientists could not agree on whether some living things, such as algae, should be classified as plants or animals. They created a third kingdom, the protist kingdom.

Sorting the Five Kingdoms

Once scientists classify living things into five kingdoms, they can sort the groups even more. For example, there are more than two million types of animals in the animal kingdom. There are more than 70,000 types of fungi in the fungi kingdom. Scientists sort each kingdom into seven groups. They are called kingdom, **phylum**, class, order, family, **genus**, and species. The species group is the most exact group that scientists use. Animals in the same species look the most alike. They can reproduce with one another. Animals of different species do not usually reproduce with one another. For example, camels and giraffes are both mammals in the animal kingdom, but they belong to different species.

1. The German shepherd dog belongs to the animal **kingdom** because it gets its energy by eating living things, it moves around, and it uses its eyes, ears, and nose to sense the world around it.

2. The German shepherd belongs to the **phylum** of animals with backbones. This is called the phylum Chordata.

3. The next group is the **class**. German shepherds belong to the class of animals that have backbones and hair and that feed milk to their young. This class is the mammal class.

4. The next group is called **order**. German shepherds belong to the order Carnivora, or carnivores. These animals eat meat.

5. The next group is called the **family**. German shepherds belong to the Canidae family. Members of this family have four pointed teeth, two in each jaw. This family includes dogs, wolves, foxes, coyotes, jackals, and hyenas.

6. German shepherds' **genus** is called *Canis*. Animals in this genus have bushy tails and long legs and hunt for food.

7. The German shepherd belongs to the **species** called *lupus*.

Sorting Yourself

When classifying yourself and your friends, you could sort yourselves by eye color, grade, or height. You could also sort yourselves by whether or not you have pets, sisters or brothers, or by your favorite books or movies.

Once you have learned to classify things, you can classify yourself and your friends. You could make up your own groups and separate your friends by age, hair color, or if they wear glasses!

In scientific classification, human beings belong to the animal kingdom. They are grouped in the phylum of Chordata and in the class of animals called mammals. You could get a grown-up to help you use the scientific system of classification.

No matter how you use classification, it will help you organize and study living and nonliving things. It is an important way for people to discover how they are connected to all things on Earth.

Glossary

carnivores (KAR-nih-vorz) Animals that eat other animals.

container (kun-TAY-ner) A box that holds things.

fungi (FUN-jy) Plantlike living things that do not have leaves, flowers, or green color, and that do not make their own food.

genus (JEE-nus) A large group of closely related plants or animals.

habitat (HA-bih-tat) The surroundings where an animal or a plant naturally lives.

herbivores (ER-bih-vorz) Animals that eat only plants.

insectivores (in-SEK-tih-vorz) Animals that eat insects for food.

invertebrates (in-VER-tih-brits) Animals without backbones.

mammals (MA-mulz) Warm-blooded animals that have backbones and hair, breathe air, and feed milk to their young.

microscopic (my-kreh-SKAH-pik) Very small.

omnivores (OM-nih-vorz) Animals that eat plants and animals.

oxygen (OK-sih-jen) A gas that has no color, taste, or odor and is necessary for people and animals to breathe.

phylum (FY-lum) One of the main parts of the animal kingdom.

prey (PRAY) An animal that is hunted by another animal for food.

reproduce (ree-pruh-DOOS) Have babies.

species (SPEE-sheez) A single kind of living thing. All people are one species.

vertebrates (VER-tih-brits) Animals that have backbones.

Index

Web Sites

Due to the changing nature of Internet links, PowerKids Press has developed an online list of Web sites related to the subject of this book. This site is updated regularly. Please use this link to access the list:

www.powerkidslinks.com/lsl/classify/